THE SMOKEHOUSE BOYS

D1601473

THE SMOKEHOUSE BOYS

Shaunna Oteka McCovey

Heyday Books, Berkeley, California

Heyday Books would like to acknowledge, for their generous contributions to our California Indian publishing program, Barbara Jean Berensmeier, Lawrence E. Crooks, Patricia A. Dixon, Ernest Siva, and Taeko Tomioka.

© 2005 by Shaunna Oteka McCovey

All rights reserved. No portion of this work may be reproduced or transmitted in any form or by any means, electronic or mechanical, including photocopying and recording, or by any information storage or retrieval system, without permission in writing from Heyday Books.

Heyday Books, founded in 1974, works to deepen people's understanding and appreciation of the cultural, artistic, historic, and natural resources of California and the American West. It operates under a 501(c)(3) nonprofit educational organization (Heyday Institute) and, in addition to publishing books, sponsors a wide range of programs, outreach, and events.

To help support Heyday or to learn more about us, visit our website at www.heydaybooks.com, or write to us at P.O. Box 9145, Berkeley, CA 94709.

Library of Congress Cataloging-in-Publication Data
McCovey, Shaunna Oteka.
  The smokehouse boys / Shaunna Oteka McCovey.
    p. cm.
  ISBN 1-59714-019-8 (pbk. : alk. paper)
  1. Indians of North America—Poetry. 2. California, Northern—Poetry. I. Title.
  PS3613.C3835S66 2005
  811'.6--dc22

                              2005017536

Cover art by Louisa D. McConnell, Yurok tribal member with Hupa and Karuk ancestry
Book design by Rebecca LeGates
Printing and Binding: McNaughton and Gunn, Saline, MI

Orders, inquiries, and correspondence should be addressed to:
        Heyday Books
        P. O. Box 9145, Berkeley, CA 94709
        (510) 549-3564, Fax (510) 549-1889
        www.heydaybooks.com

Printed in the United States of America

10 9 8 7 6 5 4 3 2 1

for my family, pyer wer si chek
especially for the Yurok, Karuk, and Hupa people
remember your beauty
return to ceremony

CONTENTS

Upriver
Creation Story I • 3
Katamiin • 4
The Dance Dress • 5
The Brush Dance Boy Lives in Phoenix, Arizona • 6
I Still Eat All of My Meals with a Mussel Shell • 7
Dreams of Wovoka • 9
The Smokehouse Boys • 10
I Would Speak • 12
Higher Medicine • 13
Coyote, It Seems • 15
The Root • 16
Still • 17
The Only Auntie Birdy We'll Ever Have • 19
Religious Freedom? • 21

Across the River
Measurements • 25
Crank • 26
Blackberry Wine • 28
Explanation for the Way I Wear My Hair • 29
Mother's Day (Welfare Day) • 30
Burying the Bones • 31
Love, Heroin • 32
Declaration • 33
Little Secret • 34
Ferris Wheel • 35
Blue-Eyed Indian Boy • 36

Food Stamps • 37

Supply Creek • 38

Intervention • 40

Disclosure • 41

At Dinner That Night • 43

Downriver

Creation Story II • 46

111 (one-eleven) • 47

Symphony No. 95546 • 48

The Fast • 52

Sweathouse Wood • 53

Clearing the Camp • 54

The Last Wild Indian • 55

Variations of Indian Love • 56

Indomitable • 59

Coyote Tails • 60

Maidenhair (Fern) • 62

Flying Geese (Tattoo) • 63

About the Author • 64

UPRIVER

Where Love Begins

Creation Story I

It began upriver
at Katamiin
where the people
danced themselves
into existence,

danced themselves
right out of the ground
into this world
of love
and hope
and loss,
and love
and hope
and loss,

and love...

Katamiin

What I remember
about the
center of the world
is that we danced there,
no matter the objection
of those who thought
it not proper, or
traditional.

Its mechanized burial
was our burial,
its unearthing
by our strong hands
was re-birth,

a starting over.
We brush dance
at Katamiin

because the Ikxaréeyavs
said it was so.
And the might
of a bulldozer
does not equal
the will of
ten thousand years.

The Dance Dress

I become my true self
through Abalone's lyric,
the rhythm of seashells dancing
on my calves, my shins.

Through this lens
I am salmon bounding over falls,
the weight of the dress
no longer an obligation, and
suddenly I know all my trails.

I am oblivious to the present,
captured by the past.
A swallow's tail floating
on currents of pedagogy and prayer.

I am fluid grace,
turning to the right,
turning back,
rising,
falling.

The dress and I
become beauty's tale,
splendor in firelight
and I glisten as
medicine crackles in my ear.

The Brush Dance Boy
Lives in Phoenix, Arizona
for Louisa Debrose McConnell

Sing me songs
of smoke and root,
in full regalia, abalone swaying,
pull your arrows from
a quiver made of me.

Tonight I went outside
and for the first time
since I've been in this
place far from home
the stars shone brighter
than the city lights,
the earth stopped still
for just one moment and I saw
the Brush Dance Boy
dancing in the full moon,
watching over me
like he has always done.

Sing me dreams
of smoke and root,
feel the sun rise in my heart
after the morning dance,
jump center into my soul.

I Still Eat All of My Meals with a Mussel Shell

Creation stories
thespiritbeings
have long been disputed
emergedfrom
by theories of
theground
evolution and
atKenek
strait crossings.

Because our rivers
halfbreedshave
were once filled
agodthatis
with gold,
neitherIndian
our women were violated
norwhite
in the worst imaginable way.

Only a few
prayersgo
still know
unheardwhen
the formula that
notspokenin
will bring the salmon
ournativetongue
up the river.

If you cannot see
istilleat
between the lines
allofmymeals
then your collected facts
witha
will never constitute
musselshell
knowledge.

Dreams of Wovoka

In search of nothing more than peace
I awake, startled, to say the least
and find Wovoka up against my door,
in his hand, a metaphor.

Poor early bird
songbird of pain,
first come, first served
leaves little gained.
Your war-torn insides will not mend…

…until

you ghost dance, ghost dance and send
those who would disturb your sleep
across the ocean, ocean deep.

The Smokehouse Boys
for Beez, Jumper, Jake, Ross, Delmer and Boyd

1 part smoke,
2 parts shadow,
1 part whispering wind,
2 parts sharpshooter,
½ singers of old Deerskin Dance songs.

They call them the Smokehouse Boys,
hanging out by the smokehouse is one of their joys.

Reach in the water, pull it up and in,
white bellies flopping, shining skin,
it must not drown in the thin night air,
a quiet thump ends all despair.

They call them the Smokehouse Boys,
for whom salmon change their shape.

1 part antler-hanging,
2 parts heart-eating,
3 parts spotlighter,
½ hero.

They call them the Smokehouse Boys,
and they carry their dreams home on their backs.

It races across the ridge like a ghost,
the one that got away, they'll boast,
was white and had red gleaming eyes,
but what they saw was no surprise,

because they are the Smokehouse Boys,
and sacred animals are drawn to them.

2 parts mountain,
2 parts river,
2 parts hot-headed warrior,
½ lovers of Indian women.

They call them the Smokehouse Boys,
for whom women give more than their hearts.

Find a bowl, pack it tight,
light it up, pass it right,
the only clear thinking is unclear,
the only thinking place is right here.

And you'll find them after the first rain,
somewhere down by the smokehouse.

I Would Speak
in honor of Georgiana Trull

I can't speak my language,
but I can name you the animals,
I can ask you for the time,
and when you feed me
I know how to say
thank you.

If you start to slow down
I can tell you to hurry up,
when clouds begin to leak
I can tell you it's raining.

If I knew how to say
I am grateful
for every word,
for every phrase,
I would speak.

If I knew how to say
without our language
we cannot be
Yurok people,
I would speak.

Higher Medicine

I am drawn to higher medicine
the way moving water
is forever drawn to its ending.
I chase Coyotes

because I have nothing to hide,
because everything has a new shape
and shadow in the moon's silky light.

I am moved by higher medicine
the way my words

                    to me   move
        back   in
way   circles
        eventual   and
            their   make

I chase Coyotes

because they hold the mystery,
because every glance is an invitation
to see more than I did before.

I need higher medicine
the way sacred rocks need to tell their stories
that begin and end, and begin again.
I chase Coyotes

because they cry old tears,
because I love the smell of warm rain
almost as much as they do.

I chase Coyotes
because I'm drawn to higher medicine
and songs sung in dreams
I only wish I could remember.

Coyote, It Seems

Coyote, it seems
you can tempt the rain,
call it by its true name,
make its meaning change

in a house made with stones
full of stories.

And Coyote, it seems
you mold sunlight with ease
into powerful beings
whose shapes cannot be seen

unless warmed by
the edge of a cloud.

And Coyote, it seems
there are tales of you told
by those who did not know
you stole fire to keep others from the cold.

And perhaps you are not
such a trickster after all.

The Root
for my sister, Julia

I'll weave
with good intention

the story of our lives,
my heart speaks,

without invention,
of how I know

where we belong,
in our place of

Snake's Nose and Swallow's Tail,
of bleached beargrass

and maidenhair,
of love designed

by our own hands,
held so resolutely

by the root that is you.

Still

I'm trying to figure out
what about you
makes me want to
sit still,
breathe deep,
plant something,
watch it grow.

I'm used to movement,
migration from here
to there,
rooting, uprooting,
collecting things,
giving it all away,
starting over again.

What about you
stifles the wanderlust,
slows the blurred seasons
I charged through?
I hurried past life
feeling as if I was
supposed to arrive
at something spectacular,
and forgot about
acknowledging
the journey.

I wish I understood
what about you
makes me want to
give you my heart,
render it listless,
count each beat,
until it is still.

The Only Auntie Birdy We'll Ever Have

Uknîi,
(I'm going to tell you a story)
about the only Auntie Birdy we'll ever have.
It began at Panaminik, where
ifápíit kunthíinati (they had a young girl).
Chavúra tá xára xasik keechíkyav uthíinati,
pamukun'ifápíit (After a long time passed
the girl was in love, and had a sweetheart.)
His name was Jack, and Jack was a good man.
Xás pa'ávansa ník xuus u'éethti pamukeechíkyav
(He took good care of his sweetheart), Auntie Birdy.
Póomahti (He looked at her) with love
every day that they were together, and
you never saw one without the other.

Chavúra tá xára. Axíich tá kunthíinati. Vúra
yâamach kunkupa'íinahiti (Finally, after a while,
they had a child and lived a very nice life.)
They called their boy Meadow Mouse,
and he was something to see.
Soon, they moved to Mount Shasta and
chavúra tá kéech pamukún'arama
(Meadow Mouse grew up), became
handsome before their eyes, and
Auntie Birdy was proud.

One day they came home to Panaminik,
then to Grandma's house on Pine Street.
"Púya'if!" Auntie Birdy would laugh,
as her nieces and nephews ran
in and out of the house.

"I'm proud of you," she'd say, "and
don't you kids forget that I am
the only Auntie Birdy you'll ever have."

The only Auntie Birdy we'll ever have
left us yesterday and xás uvâaram
(so did Jack), and xás uvâaram
(so did her Meadow Mouse), left
to meet the Ikxaréeyavs (Spirit People).
Their love for one another
even death could not separate.
So go on to Arutâanahitihirak (Indian Heaven)
Meadow Mouse, vaa pananu'avkam va'ivapuhsas
(the old ones who went before are waiting), and

go on to Arutâanahitihirak (Indian Heaven), Jack,
our Auntie Birdy and her Meadow Mouse
cannot go on without you, and

to Arutâanahitihirak (Indian Heaven) you go,
the only Auntie Birdy we'll ever have.
We'll look for you in the Milky Way
and know that you are the
brightest dancing star.

Kupanakanakana.

Religious Freedom?

The supreme law of the land is this:
if sacred lands lie
within government lands,
they are no longer sacred
and in the government's hands.

Lyng emits injudicious disgraces,
our religion means nothing
in the stern, blank faces
of the Court and their exceptional ruse,
we Indians, they opine, are but sad fools.

So what is a poor Yurok, Karuk or Tolowa to do?
Find a comfortable place at the end of the pew.

ACROSS THE RIVER

The Search for Love

Measurements

Being three sheets to the wind,
she was twice as likely
to talk about how
she wanted to be a

Super Yurok Indian Girl,
wanted to save somebody,
or the world, but couldn't
because she was

one-fourth Hupa,
one-eighth Karuk,
usually half shot,
always having to choose.

Her partially filled glass of
cheap wine:
half empty.

Her huckleberry pie: eaten alone,
sliced into sixteenths
to feel more full.

Her loves: didn't last. She made it
only four-fifths of the way
to the moon.

Her life: a series of measurements
without any sense of what it means
to be whole.

Crank

He had a beautiful smile. You know the kind, like
cream rising to the top, like
shine on chrome, like
bait on a hook.
But that was before the shrunken face,
the blanched skin, the picked sores, the
protrusion of rotting teeth.
Before the crank, he was a brushdancer.

She was a weaver. Put sticks and root in her hand
and watch miracles unfold, like
virgin apparitions, like
gold rush survival, like
old bones coming home.
But that was before the parties all night,
the sleeping around, the addiction.
Before the evolution of a bag ho.

He was unashamed. So what if he
was attracted to men, like
tides to the moon, like
opposites, like
fish to water.
But that was before the dirty names,
the condemnation, the family denial.
Now it's better to be a druggie than a fag.

She was a good mother. There
for her kids, like
tee-ball games, like
home-cooked meals, like

showing up at school-year events.
But that was before the slinging crank,
the instant cash, the hocked jewelry.
Before she started killing her own people.

They had pride. Held on to the old ways, like
hanging nets, like
carving canoes, like
stick games and listening to elders.
But that was before the crank,
before they stopped giving a shit,
before their culture started
dying right in front of them.

Blackberry Wine

Grandma slammed the bottle
down on the table, and
it burst
into a wind of
green shards
caught in candlelight,
floating, then
vanishing into the night.

She slumped in her chair,
speech slurred,
and ordered me to clean
the purple stain
from her dress,
from the splintered floor,
from my memory.

Explanation for the Way I Wear My Hair

Our love was
braided, unbraided,
sometimes wrapped
in otter skins,

or styled
with bear grease,
shiny and
smelling wild,

every so often
washed in
wild lilac,
sweet fragrance lingering,

finally wearing off.
Then it tangled, twisted,
hurt when I
tried to comb through

the knots, the
matted nest,
the split ends,
the split,

the end,
cropped bluntly
in declaration
of my mourning.

Mother's Day (Welfare Day)

They give her that
pull yourself up
by those soiled bootstraps
old look
every time she cashes
her small check.

She didn't intend to be poor,
to be stared at
or judged,
she wasn't always
living without pride.

She didn't mean for her babies
to all scream for
ice cream,
and run wild up and down
the store aisles.

Still they gave her that
your man must be worthless
tired look,
and she didn't have
the strength to protest.

At least not this Mother's Day:
this woman's work is
never done,
and it starts all over again
every first day of the month.

Burying the Bones

How can you not know
those feelings of darkness
lying upon the window sill
vanish with morning's light?

What is it that keeps
shadows dancing before you,
ever present, even in the midst
of Sunday smiles?

If only this life were
enough to sustain you,
to keep you satisfied,
content,

so you wouldn't want to
look away from love,
wouldn't have to
bury it in the backyard

like some ol' rez dog
who doesn't know
when the next meal is
and hoards his bones

but never feeds himself,
just keeps them
for the sake
of keeping them.

Love, Heroin

You think you can keep me
beyond your reservation borders,
away from your loving families
with your river-rock will,
but I'm slicker than that, bitch.

There is always a back door,
some dumb Indian who will let me
creep in so I can rape and pillage,
you know the deal.
History repeats.

Don't try to act like you're innocent,
like you never rode the Horse,
like you Indian fucks are too good
for me and what I got.
Remember the car in the alley?

Alcohol ain't got nothing on me.
I'll string you out then string you up,
I'm a noose around your pencil neck.
I got your relatives screaming for more.
Love, Heroin.

Declaration

Death
and
alcohol
are frequent
reservation lovers.

Now
only
a
fool believes
in
one
without
the other.

Little Secret

You think you can
rub me dirty
with fat, splayed fingers

and I am supposed
to learn to trust
any other attempt at affection.

You are everywhere:
my mother's brother,
my cousin's auntie,

my father's uncle
who went away to school
and came back different.

Came back with
a little secret and
whispered in my ear,

tousled my hair,
pinched my cheeks,
told me not to tell.

You think you can
tuck away sin,
leave it behind trailer doors,

as if it did not promise
to make its way back
and thoroughly destroy you.

That's the thing about
little secrets:
they always find their way home.

Ferris Wheel

Walking up our dirt road,
head hung slightly,
you'd been gone
a week or ten days,
or fourteen, it's hard
to remember exactly.

Clothes on the porch
in green trash bags,
we begged her not to
but she did it anyway.

Cyclonic was our love,
a Ferris wheel spinning;
you left, you came home,
'round and 'round
'til I was sick
and mad at you.

Then you tickled feet,
made us laugh,
and we forgot about
missing you,

you were home,
things felt good again,
we got back on
that crazy ride, full knowing,
we got back on,
went 'round and 'round,

until I felt sick...

Blue-Eyed Indian Boy

Little Indian boy
with big blue eyes
you are not a freak,
but the recipient of
one of those recessive genes
that makes you no less Indian
than the little F.B.I.
who called you an F.B.O.
You see, he doesn't know a thing
about D.N.A.,
but he knows everything about
P.A.I.N.

Food Stamps

My mother, in her youth,
thought she could pay
for our restaurant meal
with multicolored food stamps
picked up at the county
welfare agency.

It appeared logical,
buying food with food stamps.
Seemed reasonable to think
they held monetary value.
It made sense
until every patron
in that greasy diner
laughed.

Supply Creek

Call 'em crazy nights
parked up near
Supply Creek, drinkin'.

That time I fell out of the truck,
watched the back wheel
roll toward my head

in slow motion.
I wonder how many times
death took a look

and kept on movin',
how many times
she was tempted

to snuff my fire
simply because
I was stupid?

My limbs don't shudder
when I think of her now.
She's been around

enough of my life
that I almost
want to call her—friend.

But not yet,
not this steady burnin' flame.

A crumpled car
can leave my auntie broken
(she's got a friend),

the weight of years
can wear my grandma down
(she's got a friend),

but I survived Supply Creek
and a hundred more
just like it.

There's just gotta be
somethin' in store,
some grand plan.

Intervention

"I drank to drown my pain, but my damned pain learned how to swim."—Frida Kahlo

It seems your only peace
came from knowing
how to soak yourself
in misery,

wet and drowned
like an animal who
fought instinct and
forgot how to swim.

I tried to intervene,
did my best
to absorb the
oh so tragic music

you called guilt.
And for what?
I speak of you
in soft past tense

as if you
are not here
sitting beside me
on the lumpy couch.

Without a doubt,
old man,
you will be my
greatest failure.

Disclosure

When I think of how cruel
the world can be,
I want to be Neruda

and write a Great Wall
of love sonnets to stand
against the painful wind.

I want to be the salmon
who swims up the river first
to keep you from the net,

so that my white belly, caught,
offers enough warning
and you turn away in time.

I want to be the spawning grounds you return to;
the life and the death.

But you are the acorn rock,
and I am the pestle.
We grind our love into meal

and I hoard it like
the selfish poet who
saves the best words for herself,

like the woodpecker who
loves his blood-red scalp
more than the tree that feeds him.

I am an old pinêefich
who used my eyes to trick you,
told you I was magical,

and convinced you to believe
I could somehow save you
from me, from my ways.

At Dinner That Night

As you serve me
lie after lie, upon lie
piled with lies,
with a stolen spoon

I sneak an hors d'oeuvre fork
under the table and
carve the word "Skin"
into my leg,

watch blood run
warm to my ankle,
feel it absorbed by
my cheap cotton socks,

and smile inward
so you can't see
that my small ceremony
has protected me,
keeps me defiant.

DOWNRIVER

Where Love Begins Again

Creation Story II

It began downriver
at Kenek
where the people
sang themselves
into existence,

sang themselves
right out of the ground
into this world
of love
and hope
and loss,
and love
and hope
and loss,

and love...

111 (one-eleven)

They said you were ugly
sleeping on my face,
a symbol of my rite of passage,
turned into a mark of
my place in their society,

so you vanished
and I adopted a different
standard of beauty,
but now you stir

beneath my skin,
I hear you calling
and some have answered,
some have the courage

to call you their own
like I want to,
like I need to
reclaim what is mine.

Symphony No. 95546
for my mother

Spring
We planted our garden on the side of the hill behind our
house. Our corn emerged into the sunlight, and the lemon
cucumbers sprouted tall. Birds sang hymns I'd never before
heard, while you pruned your rosebushes and weeded the
flowerbeds. The dogwoods bloomed, and in the afternoons
we picked you bouquets of foxgloves as we walked up the
driveway from the schoolbus stop. The sounds of spring
were overwhelming. Every little noise, every clatter became
a note in the Creator's orchestra.

Life was a reservation symphony.

We were always musical,
while you remained
amused in the shadows. You
hid your talent for fear that you
would steal the limelight, and
willingly gave it to us—though
it was rightfully yours.

I hammer on the piano, slam
my fingers clumsily in an attempt
to create anything that resembles excellence.
I get my determination from you.
My will to make something out of nothing
must have trickled through
our shared umbilical cord.

Summer

Running water reminds me of the days we used to walk to
the creek. Sweat tickled the back of my neck as we followed
you up the trail to our swimming hole. You spread your
blanket on the bank in the shade of the young redwood tree
that became like a brother to us. We built small dams and
tested our lung capacity under the icy water. You sat quietly
and read.

I could hold my breath forever back then.

I return to the comfort of memory
when waves of loneliness and
fear consume me,
when you are not near enough
to rub the tears from my dampened face.
When all I want is to return to the safety of your womb
and start all over again.

I tear at the guitar strings while
my confused fingers bleed with
each frenzied chord.
You created a wanderer, Mother,
an ancestral song chasing
clouds across the endless sky,
a child who drifts between two worlds
both unsure and excited
about what is next to come.

Fall

The graceful swish of the river takes me back to the countless
hours spent fishing for steelhead below our house. I can still
feel the warm water wrapped around my legs, can still see
your line stretched tightly, your pole bent. You somehow

always managed to catch the biggest fish. Luck of the Irish, I used to think, but now I know differently. You were a more skilled angler, had a better sense of where the fish were, what they wanted to eat, and no matter what kind of Indian medicine I thought I had, you outfished me. You outfished us all.

Love was a river.

I am a salmon, Mother.
I was spawned in the third largest
hole in our creek, and
I show myself in human form
so that you may know
something about our people,
that you may know you are sacred
just as I am sacred.

Though my tone is steady,
I yearn for the world to hear my scream.
I need to tell Indian stories,
to make believers
out of those who doubt us.
I need you to hear me, Mother.

Winter
My baby sister cried when she found out that you were not Indian, had not been born along the river. But her tears were not derived from shame or embarrassment. She cried because she knew it would be hard for you to stay. She cried because she wanted others to accept you, to love you like she did. She cried because she was afraid of losing you to prejudice, and because, even in her tender years, she knew the reservation wouldn't be so kind.

But you stayed. You always stayed.

Without knowing it, Mother,
you created your own symphony,
your own elaborate composition.
You made use of your children's voices,
of the world around you, and
wrote a masterpiece.

You wrote the overture,
you wrote the crescendo,
you wrote it all, Mother.

You wrote it all.

The Fast

No longer will I live
on the outside
looking in,

after ten days
sipping on
acorn water and

faith

I am on the
inside looking out
and the world

is beautiful.
Sad.
Balanced.

Sweathouse Wood

This poem is for you,
Yurok man,
it's time to gather
your sweathouse wood,

time to train,
go high into the mountains,
get your head straight,
time to pray.

Go back to the sweathouse,
Karuk man,
take all of the
young men with you,

live right, tell stories,
purify yourself,
get clean, go and fast
like never before.

You know what to do,
Hupa man,
get rid of that
bad medicine,

pack rock, play sticks,
make good luck, no more waiting.
It's time to gather
that old sweathouse wood.

Epilogue
They are beginning to go back.

Clearing the Camp

While you cleared the camp
of sticker bushes, poison oak,
I prayed that you would not
cut your Chaco-sandal-exposed toes
with that rickety weed whacker

because I couldn't bear to see injury
keep you from the dance,
prevent you from your duty,
your responsibility, your part
in making the world over again.

You brought us wood,
we made you black coffee,
grounds floating and spinning
as you stirred in two heaping
spoonfuls of sugar.

You packed flint,
we fed you roasted elk,
tender from the hours spent
on our sacred fire, together
we sliced open the heavens

and balanced the weight
with arms muscled and sinewy,
shoulders strengthened by prayer.

The Last Wild Indian

He says he's
tired of hangin' around
all of those
hang-around-the-
fort Injuns
with their short hair
and choking ties, says
he's the last of his kind:
Ishi 2004,
the wild Indian of Morek
reincarnated,
always looking for
prayer seats,
places to hide,
chasing the past,
running backward
straight through time.

He says he's more of the
circle-the-wagons kind,
a Tsewenaldin Jim,
a Captain Jack,
all of the Chilula
born again,
he's Redwood Creek
before the massacre,
the baby alive on
Indian Island,
waiting for Wovoka,
for a ghost dance
of the mind.

Variations of Indian Love

Two Black Eyes and a Hickey
I hit because I don't know
how to say I'm terrified
of losing you.
I hit because you are
one more loss I cannot bear.
I hit because my grandfather
was pummeled in boarding school
and he beat my father,
who slapped my mother, and
they both spanked the shit out of me.

I kiss you so hard
that blood vessels
burst in your neck,
my lips leaving
a purplish smear
marking my territory.
If I can't make
my mark on the world
I'll make it
on your neck,
and when you go away
for the weekend
everyone will know
you are mine.

Forty Ounces of Budweiser and the Rolling Stones
Mick's lips and my hips
keep you coming back
for more, cruisin' through

this low-lit town, evading
detection and your wife
in a 1972 beast of burden,
don't want to let
the fish out of the net,
people talk on this rez,
especially to avoid
the thrust of
their own rumor mill,
the grinding down of
reputation and pride.

We drink to our affair,
forty ounces of
emotional rescue,
forty ounces of
wild horses,
seven inches of
brown sugar, and
I am merely reacting
to this life,
with no plan
but the advent
of tomorrow.

A Costco Card and Monogamy
We drive two hours,
get our groceries
for the month,
I sit close to you
all the way.

We hold hands,
refer to our list,
peruse aisles,
feast on samples
of meats and cheeses.
You need new socks,
I want bath towels,
that big screen tv
sure looks nice.

The kids need bunk beds,
school's about to start,
one more summer dance
to attend, our house
on the river
could use new paint,
but maybe next year.
Let's sit out on the deck and
watch the kids grow.

Indomitable
for MCS

There you were, wilted,
as any flower would be,
having just weathered death's hard rain.

A gaping hole left
where your heart called home,
innocence buried

with them
and what they
left behind.

The fear, the isolation
of not knowing
why. Why?

Yet fleeting breath
could not quell life's desire
to love without paralysis.

And you found it,
perhaps where you
least expected.

In a milieu of laughter,
of acceptance
near the river's edge.

You are a rock among stones,
the heartbreak that remembered
how to love,

the wound that bled and cried,
and left a fading scar.
You are their beauty incarnate.

Coyote Tails

Coyote, tell me a little
about your wily ways,
I've got so much to learn
and am going no place in particular.

I want to be a thief of fire,
sing lonely ballads to the
Brush Dance Boy in the moon,
I want to trade you smoked salmon
for a few tricks, some acorns for a single truth.

Let's go for a ride
in your two-tone truck,
half river-green, half reservation mud,
with vanity plates announcing
"Creator of the World."

I can spot you in any crowd,
hear you coming from miles away.
I know when you are creeping up
from behind because the hair stands up
on the back of my neck,

and when I turn around to see nothing
I pretend that you are there
because I like to be tricked
and I need only one truth

that I'll get from you someday
because I'm bound to catch on
to your crazy ways
if I spend enough time
chasing after the end of your tail.

I know you, Coyote.
I saw you once in the mirror,
watched you put cream and sugar
in your coffee and say it was
a sign that times have changed

because now you prefer
your fry bread low-fat,
salmon paté instead of salmon patty,
but you are still a coyote,
and that will never change.

So whether you lead or mislead,
I'll continue to follow
because I like to be fooled
and all I need is one truth

which I'll get from you someday
because eventually I'll know
all those crazy ways
if I spend enough time
hanging on to the end of your tail.

Maidenhair (Fern)

Dark, like the color of closed eyes,
like the color of night
as it unfolds and creates patterns
that fall with heavy rain

into place. Patterns that
sleep upon steep shoulders,
that warm restless bodies
through the seasons

'til summer. Black,
like the hue of perfect shadows,
like the shade of coal tresses
brushed over, fingered-through 'til plush,

until the scent of dusk
is gathered with supple hands
eager to weave the same story
over and over.

Flying Geese (Tattoo)

Resting softly upon your skin
in angle and perfect triangle,
wings spread so vast that
they return to meet in full circle,

to enclose your secrets
braided in beargrass
burned years before
and dried to brilliant white.

You have nothing to fear,
because flying geese
forgive the one who falters.

Woven in places of prayer,
where fern and root become one,
laid in gentle design,
on the verge of full intention,

guided to exact formation
with patience, hard taught,
like learning to accept
what life takes away

then finding your way again,
because flying geese
forgive the one who forgets to fly.

About the Author

Shaunna Oteka McCovey (Yurok/Karuk) wrote her first poem at the age of six, while growing up on the Yurok Indian reservation in northern California. She holds master's degrees in social work and environmental law and a juris doctorate from Vermont Law School. Her poems have appeared in *News from Native California*, *Through the Eye of the Deer*, and *The Dirt Is Red Here*. This is her first full-length book of poetry.